# Sufi meets Sanathan

Arvind Seshadri

Published by Arvind Seshadri, 2024.

While every precaution has been taken in the preparation of this book, the publisher assumes no responsibility for errors or omissions, or for damages resulting from the use of the information contained herein.

SUFI MEETS SANATHAN

**First edition. December 25, 2024.**



ISBN: 979-8230564447

Written by Arvind Seshadri.

# Acknowledgement

Every literary work stems from the knowledge gained from reading another literary work. Reading enables thoughts that gives rise to creative endeavours. "Sufi meets Sanathan" has been possible because of the book "Forty rules of Love" by Elif Shafak. I would like to convey my sincere thanks to this renowned author who is a torch bearer for woman's rights and views across the world through her books, interviews and speeches.

I would like to thank all the great saints, philosophers and Gurus of Sanathana dharma from whom I have learnt so much directly and indirectly. I am a mere speck of dust in front of them. Just as a gust of wind carries the dust to various places of sanctity and gets purified, I am fortunate to read and listen to these timeless masters. I have just reciprocated their fountain of knowledge in my own words. I place this book at their lotus feet with a sense of deep gratitude.

Writing an essay, treatise or a book takes time and effort and without the support of friends and family, authors cannot complete their work. My wife Kavita and my two daughters Manisha and Niharika are a constant source of support and encouragement for all my activities be it my books, poems or discourses. My MBA classmate and close friend, Mrs. Sripriya Seshadri provided invaluable inputs to fine tune the book. I would like to thank them all.

Last but not the least print on demand service providers and platforms that allow me to explore various genres. Without their help none of my work would have seen the light of the day.

# Introduction

As someone who enjoys Sufi musical renditions of Kabir's Dohe, the mystic and poet who lived in India in the early part of the 14<sup>th</sup> century, reading Shams of Tabriz's rules on Sufi Mysticism was profoundly fulfilling. The Dervish who transformed the Intellectual Jalalluddin Rumi into a poet. Shams' rules resonated deeply, echoing principles from our scriptures especially the three spiritual paths of Gnana Marga, Karma Marga and Bhakti Marga as propagated by the three great Acharyas that this land has witnessed namely Adi Shankaracharya, Ramanujacharya and Madhwacharya.

I could see the similarity and the underlying meaning of the phrases, vividly showing the oneness between religions and the oneness of the divine. It showed that when you are enlightened, your soul beats the same, irrespective of whether you are in Konya (The city that made Rumi) or Kaaladi (The Village that gave us Adishankara).

According to Shams, the Quran has multiple layers of interpretation, likewise the Bhagwad Gita also offers various levels of understanding. It is, after all, the sermon delivered by the Lord himself. The more one delves deeper into it, one will unearth pearls of wisdom. Adi Shankara propagated the method of Knowledge as a way to experience the divine, Ramanuja propagated the method of Action as a way to the divine and Madhwacharya propagated the method of Devotion as a way to experience the divine. This book is an attempt to compare the two schools of thought – Sufism and Sanaathana Dharama to bring out the similarities and collective wisdom. It would show that we are all walking towards the same goal but the walking sticks are in different shapes and sizes.

When we finally see the inner light all the sticks would disappear and we would be one with the divine.

## The Forty Rules of Love

Elif Shafak is the torch bearer for the Mystic of Sufism in the modern world mixing contemporary story telling with the nuances of Sufism that enthrals her readers. It also enables her to be the voice of the unheard and under privileged to create an inclusive wholesome society that rises beyond caste, creed, race or religion.

Elif Shafak has beautifully woven the tenets of Sufi Mysticism with a women's quest for true love in this wonderful fiction, "The Forty Rules of Love". Beyond the literary sophistication exhibited by Shafak, what intrigued me in the 40 rules was the message.

As a person who believes in his religion and uses it to elevate his spiritual journey, I believe that every religion is striving to elevate the spiritual quotient in an individual.

Some people may criticize Elif Shafak for trying to be preachy and justifying the acts of a women's extra-marital relationship but for me I delved deeper into the rules to extract the underlying meaning. I was not too much worried about the messenger but the message. Every rule I read was Deja vu. It was something that I knew and / or practiced subconsciously. These were the rules taught to us through our scriptures and explained by our enlightened gurus.

The following pages will discuss each rule as stated by Shams and an equivalent anecdote from Hinduism, Buddhism or Jainism or verses from our Hindu scriptures that reflects the same perspective. I am hoping that readers of this book, see the unity in duality which could possibly help them in their own spiritual journey. They don't need to switch sides or berate one against the other as the ultimate destination will be eventually reached.

*'Aakashath Pathitham Thoyam Yatha Gachathi Sagaram*

*Sarvadeva Namaskaram Keshavam Prathi Gachathi'*

As the water that falls down in rain from anywhere in the sky finally reaches the Ocean, the worship of any divine aspect ultimately reaches the Supreme Being.

Adishankara

## <u>Shams - Rule 1</u>

**How we see God** *is a direct reflection of how we see ourselves. If God brings to mind mostly fear and blame, it means there is too much fear and blame welled inside us. If we see God as full of love and compassion, so are we.*

Even in Sanathana Dharma, we believe that the mind of the individual determines his perception about God. Bhakti Marga or the path of devotion is exemplified through the fourth Avatar (incarnation) of Vishnu – Narasimha. Vishnu is known as The Preserver in the Hindu Trinity that also consists of Brahma – The Creator and Shiva – The Destroyer. Vishnu came in the form of a Lion Headed Man to kill the demon king Hiranyakashipu. His son Prahlad was the foremost devotee of Vishnu and the king tried various ways to threaten and kill his son for worshipping his sworn enemy Vishnu, but he survived. Prahlad saw in Vishnu the Benevolent Protector but Hiranyakashipu saw Vishnu as a Sorcerer. Hiranyakashipu had raging anger towards Vishnu, who appeared in the form of an angry Lion Man and consumed him.

As we can see Hiranyakashipu saw God as a Wilful evil Sorcerer whom he disliked and God appeared before him just as he perceived. Prahlad always saw Narsimha as the epitome of courage and compassion and hence he was protected by him against the evil deeds of Hiranyakashipu.

The subconscious mind is a very strong tool that we underestimate most of the time. We eventually see and perceive things in the way we have envisaged them subconsciously. A rational person tries to find equations to understand god. An atheist looks for logic in religion to prove God doesn't exist. A believer simply believes in the supreme as he experiences it in his subconsciousness.

Lord Narasimha vanquishing Hiranyakashipu (Fig 1.1)

## <u>Shams - Rule 2</u>

**The Path to the Truth** *is a labour of the heart, not of the head. Make your heart your primary guide! Not your mind. Meet, challenge and ultimately prevail over your nafs (ego, psyche, soul) with your heart. Knowing your Self will lead you to the knowledge of God.*

Radhika more popularly known as Radha in our Hindu Scriptures exemplifies the above statement. She only used her heart to seek the Bhagwan or the divine. Lord Krishna reciprocated her love as he was bound by her Love and Devotion. The Ras-Lila which translate to "Sweet Acts of Krishna" involved uninhibited music and dance of the Gopikas along with Krishna. Gopikas were the girls in Gokul who were devotees and consorts of Krishna in their mind. Krishna played the flute while the Gopikas danced with gay abandon. The Gopikas and Krishna were seen as one while dancing. It was like the Yin-Yang, one could not be without the other. It is said Lord Shiva who is considered the God of Dancing was smitten by Ras-Lila, that he came down to see it. It is similar to the Dance of the Dervishes who are in active meditation seeking the divine with their continuous Whirling.

Whether you are a Devi or Dervish, with love in your heart, music in your lips and dance in your action, you will become one with the divine.

Radha & Krishna (Fig 1.2)

## <u>Shams - Rule 3</u>

**You can study God through everything and everyone in the universe**, *because God is not confined in a mosque, synagogue or church. But if you are still in need of knowing where exactly His abode is, there is only one place to look for him: in the heart of a true lover.*

In Hinduism, it is firmly believed that God is everything from the Microcosm to the Macrocosm. It is depicted in the Vamana Avatar of Lord Vishnu. Vamana means a dwarf. Vishnu comes as a dwarf seeking alms and asks King Mahabali for a piece of land measuring three steps of his feet. Without knowing who was in front of him, Mahabali agrees and Vamana transforms into **"Ulagalanda Perumal"** (The Supreme Lord who measured the three worlds). The dwarf transforms into a gigantic being and measures the Earth and Heavens with his two steps. Mahabali understood his folly and asked Vamana to place the third step on his head. When Mahabali looked into his heart, he found God.

In Hindu Philosophy, the subterranean realm beneath the earth is considered as **Pathal Lok** literally meaning below the feet. When God's Feet is on one's head, it's the greatest blessing a human can receive and Vishnu pushes Mahabali to the Pathal Lok and makes him the King of the Underworld.

The Hindu scriptures explain the subtlety of the migration of Vishnu from the Supreme Being to one confined inside the four walls of a temple using the five states of Vishnu – *Para Vasudevan, Vyuhah Vasudevan, Vibhava Vasudevan, Antharyami, Archai.*

**Para Vasudevan** - is the Transcendental Supreme, the driving force.

**Vyuhah Vasudevan** - the one who manifests into the creator and protector.

**Vibhava Vasudevan** - is the different incarnations of Lord Vishnu in the different *Yugas* (Different eons of time) to build righteous order. There are 4 Yugas in Hindu Philosophy. Sathya Yuga or Kritha Yoga, Tretha Yuga, Dvapara Yuga, and Kali Yuga. Each cycle characterized by the reduced timeline of each Yuga.

**Antharyami** - is the one within us driving our soul and every act we perform

**Archai**- is the one who is worshipped in different forms in the temple.

In Hinduism, Kali Yuga represents the current era, marked by spiritual darkness, but it also holds potential for spiritual growth and awakening. Man, Women or Child, you can look without and learn about the divine or look within and seek the divine. Either way you will find him.

Vamana (Fig 1.3)

## <u>Shams - Rule 4</u>

**Intellect and love are made of different materials.** *Intellect ties people in knots and risks nothing, but love dissolves all tangles and risks everything. Intellect is always cautious and advises, 'Beware too much ecstasy', whereas love says, 'Oh, never mind! Take the plunge!' Intellect does not easily break down, whereas love can effortlessly reduce itself to rubble. But treasures are hidden among ruins. A broken heart hides treasures.*

The above rule resonates directly with an incident that relates to Lord Krishna, the Supreme being. Before the beginning of the Kurukshetra war, Lord Krishna who was related to both the Pandavas and Kauravas, the two warring clans, was bound to give something to each of them as he couldn't be seen as partial. Arjuna and Duruyodhana the two warring cousins went to see Krishna. Arjuna was seated at Krishna's legs whereas Duryodhana was seated at his head. When Krishna opened his eyes, he saw Arjuna first and hence gave him the right to ask first. Arjuna said he didn't need anything except Krishna. Duryodhana was overjoyed that the fool had not asked for Krishna's army and weapons. Arjuna eventually won the war as God was with him. Duryodhana thought through the intellect and believed weapons and armies would win the war whereas Arjuna thought with his heart and chose Krishna.

Draupadi, the queen of the pandavas was being disrobed in the courtroom by Dushasana, one of the Kauravas and cousin to the Pandavas. Yudhishtir, the eldest brother of the five pandavas had lost his wife Draupadi who he had put as a bet in the game of dice between the Pandavas and Kauravas. Great Learned Men where in the courtroom but no one said a word. Draupadi didn't attempt to stop Dushasana, she simply raised her hand above her head and prayed to Lord Krishna, completely trusting her devotion to the supreme being.

Bhakti is another form of love. She risked everything and the divine saved her chastity. She surrendered to the love of the divine.

Whether on a battled field like Kurukshetra or within the battles of our mind, we will never be able to see the divine by intellectual reasoning but only through love.

Arjuna & Duryodhana with Krishna

Krishna saving Draupadi's chastity (Fig 1.4)

## <u>Shams - Rule 5</u>

**Most of the problems of the world stem from linguistic mistakes and simple misunderstanding.** *Don't ever take words at face value. When you step into the zone of love, language, as we know it becomes obsolete. That which cannot be put into words can only be grasped through silence.*

Nothing explains the power of silence better than the story of Krishna and his beloved friend Sudhama. Sudhama was in poverty and his wife asked him to go and visit Krishna, the King of Dwaraka and seek help. Sudhama came with some puffed rice stuffed in his patched-up bag. It was all he could afford.

Krishna welcomed him with open arms and treated him as if God had come to his household. In the Hindu scriptures it says *'Athithi Devo Bhava'* which translates to Guest is God. Sudhama had so much affection and love that he didn't want to trivialize the divine love for a few coins of Gold. In the evening he returned home and found a palace instead of his hut. The Palace was brimming with Gold, Diamonds, New Clothes, Tons of Grocery. He just closed his eyes. Sudhama didn't utter a word when he was in Dwaraka neither did Krishna. They spoke through their silence.

Let us not offer prayers to the divine replicating the barter trade. I offer you gifts bless me with my wish. Pray in silence to seek oneness with the divine and not for mere gold that keeps you wanting more and remain in the eternal cycle of life.

Krishna and Sudama (Fig 1.5)

## <u>Shams - Rule 6</u>

**Loneliness and Solitude** *are two different things. When you are lonely, it is easy to delude yourself into believing that you are on the right path. Solitude is better for us, as it means being alone without feeling lonely. But eventually it is best to find a person who will be your mirror. Remember only in another person's heart can you truly see yourself and the presence of God within you.*

We could rephrase the above as Loneliness and Aloneness. Loneliness creates a sense of delusion especially leading to negative consequences. Aloneness on the other hand is just being. In the "Forty rules of Love", Shams searched for Rumi and found him, just as Shabari waited for Rama and found him. Shabari was never alone even for a second in all those years she waited for Rama. She always had Rama in her heart and prayers on her lips. While living alone, she never was lonely. When Rama finally arrived, bypassing other sages to Shabari's ashram, it showed that the divine knew the right home of true love. Shabari gave Rama berries after tasting them, no one else had the privilege of giving used food to the divine and Rama accepted them gleefully.

When you are filled with the love for the divine, even the remains of a bitten fruit, taste like nectar to the Supreme being.

The Story of Shabari shows that we are never alone, as the divine is always within us as Antharyami. We just need to look within. This is endorsed by the Vedic scriptures too through the phrase **'Aham Brahmasmi'** which literally means I am the Supreme Being. A phrase that would suit Shabari to the T.

Shabari and Rama (Fig 1.6)

## <u>Shams - Rule 7</u>

**Whatever happens in your life**, *no matter how troubling things might seem,* **do not enter the neighbourhood of despair.** *Even when all doors remain closed, God will open up a new path only for you. Be thankful! It is easy to be thankful when all is well. A Sufi is thankful not only for what he has been given but also for all that he has been denied.*

Let me turn the above statement 180 degrees. We always tend to seek the Lord when things go wrong and not when things go right. We take credit when things go right and we blame God when things go wrong and ask him to rectify it. There is a beautiful story of Krishna's conversation with Kunti depicted in the Bhagwad Puran. The Bhagwad Puran is one of the eighteen puranas (Hindu literature) attributed to Veda Vyas and promotes devotion towards Krishna. Below is what Kunti says

*'Vipadaḥ santu tāḥ śaśvat tatra tatra jagad-guro*

*bhavato darśanaṁ yat syād apunar bhava-darśanam'*

'Let there be difficulties again and again, o Guru of the universe. Because (in difficulties) we may have the opportunity to see you, and this means we will not have to take birth ever again.'

Kunti, the mother of the Pandavas of the Kuru Dynasty, who lived in the Dvapara Yuga and also the aunt of Lord Krishna seeks a boon from him that she has difficulties again and again. Explaining her boon she says, only in times of difficulty we think of you. Having difficulties repeatedly will ensure I am always thinking of you. She is not worried about difficulties just as Shams says a Sufi thanks God for what he has been denied.

Kunti accepted with equanimity both the happy times and challenging times. Once we detach ourselves from the duality of the Good and Bad ( the two possible outcomes of our actions), focusing on our duties and showing our gratitude to God, we will never despair. It would lead us to the conclusion that everything that happens, happens for the good. What happened in the past, What is happening in the present and What will happen in the future are all for the good.

The above perspective is explicitly depicted in the verse from the Bhagwad Puran also known as Bhagawatham.

*'Kaayena Vaacaa Manase-Indriyair-Vaa*

*Buddhy-Aatmanaa Vaa Prakrteh Svabhaavaat*

*Karomi Yad-Yat-Sakalam Parasmai*

*Naaraayannayeti Samarpayaami'*

'Whatever actions I do with my Body, Speech, Mind or Sense Organs, or using my Intellect, Feelings of Heart or (unconsciously) through the natural tendencies of my Mind, All those, I do for the Supreme Being (without sense of attachment to the results),and I Surrender them to the Lotus Feet of Sriman Narayana.'

Kunti – Seeking the Boon (Fig1.7)

## <u>Shams - Rule 8</u>

**Patience does not mean to passively endure.** *It means to look at the end of a process. What does patience mean? It means to look at the thorn and see the rose, to look at the night and see the dawn. Impatience means to be shortsighted as to not be able to see the outcome. The lovers of God never run out of patience, for they know that time is needed for the crescent moon to become full.*

Sita's life in Ashok Vatika epitomises the above rule. Ashok Vatika was the Demon King Ravana's private mini forest in the Kingdom of Lanka. After being Kidnapped by Ravana, Sita was imprisoned in the Ashok Vatika protected by Rakshasis (demonesses).She knew Lord Ram, her husband would come for her. Even in the midst of darkness she could see light.

When the great Hanuman (Monkey God) came to find out her whereabouts, he found her in the Ashok Vatika. He introduced himself by giving Ram's ring as proof, and offered to take her back with him. Sita refused to come with him and said, 'I will wait for my Ram to come and get me.' She had the gumption and conviction about the outcome.

In our lives, we need to inculcate patience so we are able to ride both the crest and troughs of life. Understanding that it's a sinusoidal wave and this too shall pass.

Sita with Hanuman (Fig1.8)

## <u>Shams -Rule 9</u>

**East, West, South, or North makes little difference.** *No matter what your destination, just be sure to make every journey a journey within. If you travel within, you'll travel the whole wide world and beyond.*

This rule directly relates to Advaita Vedanta, the Hindu philosophy founded and propagated by Adi Shankaracharya. Adi Shankaracharya in his text ***Upadesha Sahasri*** ( A Thousand Teachings ) says the following

*I am other than name, form and action.*

*My nature is ever free!*

*I am Self, the supreme unconditioned Brahman.*

*I am pure Awareness, always non-dual.*

( Upadesha Sahasri 11.7)

The very focus of Advaita Vedanta or Advaita Philosophy is 'realization of truth'. This realization of truth is only possible by looking within and not without.

Ramana Maharishi, one of the most enlightened souls from Southern India is considered a ***Jivamukti*** literally meaning 'liberated while living'. He lived during the 19th century. His personal answers to British Author, Paul Brunton are so profound that it invokes a state of nothingness in us even today. One such statement exactly reflects the need to look within as stated in the Sufi philosophy too.

Maharishi says to Paul Brunton

*'As you get enlightenment, you will not think that it is Paul Brunton who is writing, because your consciousness will be centred in That which is beyond the little self of Paul Brunton.'*

Maharishi indirectly asks Paul Brunton to look beyond his label Paul Brunton as he is known to the world and ask the question Who am I?

Whether we are Parasuram, Paul or Parvez, we need to ask the same question of ourselves.

Adi Shankara

Ramana Maharishi

( Fig1.9)

## <u>Shams -Rule 10</u>

**The midwife knows that when there is no pain**, *the way for the baby cannot be opened and* **the mother cannot give birth**. *Likewise, for a new self to be born, hardship is necessary. Just as clay needs to go through intense heat to become strong, Love can only be perfected in pain.*

The treatise of Bhagwad Gita which is also known as the Song of God happens when the seeker is in pain. It's a direct replica of the above rule where a new self can only be born when there is pain. Arjuna is pained by seeing who is in front of him in the Kurukshetra war and he states that through the below sloka to Lord Krishna.

*'āchāryāḥ pitaraḥ putrās tathaiva cha pitāmahāḥ*

*mātulāḥ śhvaśhurāḥ pautrāḥ śhyālāḥ sambandhinas tathā*

*etān na hantum ichchhāmi ghnato 'pi madhusūdana*

*api trailokya-rājyasya hetoḥ kiṁ nu mahī-kṛite'*

I see in front of me, my teachers, my grandfather, my uncles, my nephews, other relatives, family friends their sons and other great warriors. O Madhusudhana I don't want to kill them, even if they wish to kill me. What purpose does it serve if I kill all of them and become the king of the three worlds.

Here was the greatest archer on earth in the Dvapara Yuga (Second World Cycle as per the scriptures) going into severe depression at the thought of losing loved ones.

Krishna allows Arjuna to go through this process so he can hit rock bottom. He then provides a treatise on the essence of Life, Dharma, and Arjuna's duty as a Kshatriya. On hearing the treatise Arjuna transforms from a sulking warrior to win the war for the Pandavas.

When we are in total darkness, even a small candle will fill the room with light. The trials and tribulations of life teaches us to become stronger and eventually reach a state of Paramananda (eternal bliss).

Arjuna In Distress - Seeking Krishna (Fig 2.0)

## <u>Shams - Rule 11</u>

**The quest for love changes the user.** *There is no seeker among those who search for love who has not matured on the way. The moment you start looking for love, you start to change within and without.*

Whether in love for the beloved or love for the divine, it transforms the person inside out. A beautiful anecdote in Mahabharat reflects this phenomenon. Vidura the chief advisor for the Kuru clan and half-brother of King Dhirthirashtra was considered the wisest among all. Krishna visited Vidura's household as a guest. Sulabha, Vidura's wife was overwhelmed to see Lord Krishna in her abode and as per the culture prevailing then, treated her guest with food. She was so blinded by her love and devotion for krishna that she was lost physically and mentally. She started peeling bananas throwing away the banana and offering the peel to Krishna. Krishna ate the peel with pleasure. Soon Vidura entered his home and reprimanded his wife, who now got her senses back and saw that bananas were strewn all over. She was embarrassed and ashamed of her misdemeanour.

Krishna scolded Vidura for being harsh on Sulabha and said the peel offered with Love was tastier than a fruit offered without devotion. Even the great Vidura considered one of the wisest men of those times had learnt a lesson.

Love is the pause between two notes that creates mesmerizing music. Love is the twilight that connects brightness and darkness. The body is the temple of God, hence love starts within us. Self-Love reflects on to others, it could be human or animal or even nature. Love is transformational for the lover and the loved.

Sulabha (Vidura's wife) giving peels to Krishna (Fig 2.1)

## <u>Shams - Rule 12</u>

**There are more fake gurus and false teachers in this world than the number of stars** *in the visible universe. Don't confuse power-driven, self-centred people with true mentors. A genuine spiritual master will not direct your attention to himself or herself and will not expect absolute obedience or utter admiration from you, but instead will help you to appreciate and admire your inner self. True mentors are as transparent as glass. They let the light of God pass through them.*

One of the most popular and controversial Gurus of the world popularly known as Osho said, as long as the spiritual supermarket exists, there will always be Guru's and Preachers. In today's world, religion is a business too not just a path to spiritual enlightenment. There is enough and more in the ancient scriptures to follow and learn than to go in search of a Neo Guru.

A great example to explain what a true Guru looks like is an anecdote from the Life of Vaishnavite Saint Ramanujacharya. Ramanujacharya who propagated the Vedanta Philosophy of Visishta Advaitha (qualified monism) obtained his initiation as a Sage with the secret mantra (Prayer Verse) being revealed to him by his Guru. Ramanujacharya asked him, what will happen if I reveal this Mantra to everyone, his guru said they will all get Moksha (eternal salvation) and you will go to hell. Ramanuja went on the roof of the temple and disclosed the mantra to the whole world. Ramanujacharya was not just a theologist but also a social reformer. He believed that religion was not a hegemony of the upper caste and said God does not differentiate between people and brought the so-called lower caste also into the Bhakti Marga (path of devotion).

Ramanuja believed that we have both animal instincts and divine instincts within us. It's for us to decide which we want to develop. He believed that the communication with god was through Bhakti and the experience of the Brahman (Supreme Being) would come only through the path of self-discovery.

Bhakti is the ladder that takes the soul towards the quest of the sublime. There is no greater Guru than the divine. When we cut out the outside and inside noise and pray to him, we will experience him.

Ramanujacharya – Telling the Secret Mantra to Everyone (Fig 2.2)

## Shams -Rule 13

**Try not to resist the changes, which come your way.** *Instead let life live through you. And do not worry that your life is turning upside down. How do you know that the side you are used to is better than the one to come?*

Lord Krishna himself is a great example of not resisting change. As a young boy he was full of music and dance, playful, naughty, and enjoying the adulation of the girls in Gokul. When the time came for him to go to Gurukul (Studying at the Guru's home), he went to the ashram of Sage Sandipani. Sandipani, sometimes rendered Sāndīpana, was the guru of Krishna and his brother Balarama. He educated them regarding the Vedas, the art of drawing, astronomy, medicine, training them to handle elephants and horses, and archery. Sandipani showed Krishna the real purpose of his life. Krishna before meeting Sandipani and Krishna after tutelage from Sandipani were two different people. Radha, his beloved was in Gokul and when Krishna went to Mathura from Gokul, he left his Flute with her stating, 'Dear Radhe, I don't need this anymore, you keep it.'

The transformation of Krishna from the playful cowherd to a Global Guru was complete. Krishna went on to become the King of the Yadavas and Master Strategist of the Kurukshetra war enabling the Pandavas to win the war. In the process of helping Arjuna who was the most powerful warrior among the pandavas, Lord Krishna gave the people of Kali Yuga, the Bhagwad Gita, a sermon delivered by him to Arjuna amidst the war. The treatise which teaches the human mind the real purpose of its life.

Robin Sharma, the management guru and philosopher beautifully summarizes the point about transformation in an individual. He says, 'when the pupil is ready the teacher arrives.' When we are ready to accept the change and not fight it, the fog clears and we are ready to receive inputs from the Guru that begins our journey of transformation.

Playful Child

Sincere Student

Global Guru

(Fig 2.3)

<u>**Shams -Rule 14**</u>

**God is busy with the completion of your work, both outwardly and inwardly.** *He is fully occupied with you. Every human being is a work in progress that is slowly but inexorably moving toward perfection. We are each an unfinished work of art both waiting and striving to be completed. God deals with each of us separately because humanity is fine art of skilled penmanship where every single dot is equally important for the entire picture.*

The **Dasavatharam** (Ten incarnations) of Vishnu explains this evolutionary process, which in some ways resembles Darwin's theory of evolution. It also represents the evolution of the human body and mind as each incarnation follows a sequential progression, physically, mentally, and emotionally.

It starts with the first incarnation, **Matsya** (fish). We as humans live inside water in our mother's womb. The second incarnation is that of **Koorma** (tortoise) which is akin to Birthing when the mother's water breaks and we are born. The third incarnation is that of **Varaha** (wild boar), we have entered the jungle called life. The fourth incarnation is **Narasimha** (Lion-Man). It is a stage where we have a mix of animal and human instincts combined. The fifth incarnation is **Vaamana** (Dwarf), we have evolved from animal instinct to human attributes but still small in our thinking as we get stuck in the little pleasures of life. By the fifth Avatar the human has arrived. The next five focuses on the mental transformation of the Human.

The sixth incarnation is **Parashurama** (The Warrior), the one who decimates the entire Kshatriya race as they were so much consumed by debauchery. It is the first stage of evolution into the higher state of being when we let go of all the vices. The seventh incarnation is **Rama** (The perfect man).Rama stood for righteousness and is one of the holiest of the incarnations. The eighth incarnation is that of **Bala Rama** (Man with the plough). He sows the seeds of the divine deeply into us. Metaphorically speaking, we are the seed and can't exist on our own and it is the divine that helps us germinate. The ninth incarnation is **Krishna** (God). None of the other incarnations perform miracles like Little Krishna. Lord Vishnu shows that evolution can be made from human to the divine. The last incarnation is **Kalki** (Abstract). It is to show that evolution continues as we move into the state of nothingness.

Through the Dasavatharam we can see that the Supreme Being himself is undergoing evolution from the "Aquatic to the Abstract". We humans could evolve from being a "Single cell to the Sublime" enabled by the Bhagwan (Supreme Being), both from the inside as the Antharyami and outside as The Protector.

Dasavatharam – Ten Incarnations of Vishnu (Fig 2.4)

## <u>Shams -Rule 15</u>

**It's easy to love a perfect God, unblemished and infallible that He is.** *What is far more difficult is to love fellow human being with all their imperfections and defects. Remember, one can only know what one is capable of loving. There is no wisdom without love. Unless we learn to love God's creation, we can neither truly love nor truly know God.*

Ramayana, the great epic written by Valmiki depicts the Journey of Rama. In the Ramayana, Lord Rama shows us how everyone is god's creation and needs to be embraced with love. Let us delve into the Ramayana to experience his *Karunya* (Compassion ).

As a young man, sage Vishwamithra took Rama from Ayodhya to protect his ashram and the penance of the sages against the demon Taraka. When Taraka came to attack the Sages, Rama said 'O great Rishi, how can I kill a women.' The others saw a demon in Taraka and Rama saw a woman in the demon.

After being exiled from the Kingdom for no fault of his, he undertook the arduous journey of living in the forest for fourteen years as ordered by his step mother. A lot happened during this long journey. He befriended Guha who was a Fisherman, who helped Rama, his wife Sita and his brother Lakshmana cross the Ganges, the holy river. Rama hugged Guha and called him his fourth brother besides Bharatha, Lakshmana and Shatrugna who were his step brothers. Rama never saw them as stepbrothers. They too reciprocated and respected him as the eldest Brother.

As Rama's journey continued, he befriended Sugreeva, the Monkey King and promised to avenge his defeat against his brother Vaali, who had forcibly taken away his kingdom and his wife Ruma. Rama vowed to help Sugreeva get back what he had lost and Sugreeva in turn told Rama that they would leave no stone unturned till the Vanar Sena

(Sugreeva's Army) found Sita who had been captured by the demon king Ravana. Rama forged a friendship for Life with Sugreeva.

Rama's search of Sita took him to the southern tip of India where Vibhishana, the demon prince came to meet him from Lanka seeking asylum. Vibhishana was the brother of Ravana, The King of Lanka and the most powerful man in the peninsula. Rama was on his way to Lanka to wage a war on Ravana and free his wife from captivity. When everyone around Rama suspected Vibhishana, Rama told them that he would accept Vibhishana even if he was a spy, as he had sought asylum.

Lastly when Ravana stood helpless in front of Rama bereft of all the weapons, Rama said, '**Hey Lankeshwar,** Emperor of Lanka, if you still want to fight come back tomorrow well-armed.' Indirectly indicating he was ready to pardon him right now.

Rama perceived a demoness, a person of lower caste, a monkey, a potential spy and even his sworn enemy with the same love and grace. In Rama's eyes everyone was the same.

It is a lesson for us that Rama had left behind from the Treta Yuga. Divinity is there in everything around us. Be it Mountains, Oceans, Plants, Animals, Humans or even an Alien species. We just need to have the light in our eyes and love in our heart to see it.

Rama-Taraka Rama – Guha

Rama- Sugreeva Rama – Vibishana

(Fig 2.5)

## <u>Shams -Rule 16</u>

**Real faith is the one inside.** *The rest simply washes off. There is only one type of dirt that cannot be cleansed with pure water, and that is the stain of hatred and bigotry contaminating the soul. You can purify your body through abstinence and fasting, but only love will purify your heart.*

In India, the Ganges is considered the most sacred river and the ashes of the dead are immersed in it so that the soul is purified. Ganges is considered to be the purest of all waters capable of cleansing even the soul.

The soul, when it is not part of the body is anyways pure as it only gets corrupted due to its association with the body. The bodily senses when integrated with a corrupted mind create hatred and bigotry towards another soul.

There is a concept of "Atmashuddhi" in Sanathana Dharma. It literately translates to self-purification. Atmashuddhi is attained by continuously chanting the name of the divine. There are specific Shlokas that are given in the Upanishads, a subsect of the Vedic Scriptures and in Jainism, there are poems. Some Yoga practitioners also recite these mantras before performing Yoga. The word Yoga actually comes from the word Yogam which means penance. The most important criteria for Atmashuddhi is total dedication and devotion to the divine.

The transformation of Valmiki is a great example to explain the purification of the inside. Before he became a renowned Sage, Valmiki was a dacoit. One day he is accosted by Narada, the son of Brahma, the creator. Valmiki is drawn towards him and seeks redemption from the sins he has committed. Narada felt the sincerity in Valmiki's words and asked him to recite the name "Rama". Valmiki went into a solitary location in the mountain and started his penance by constantly reciting "Mara". The word Mara means death or the devil. Valmiki being uneducated, just kept reciting Mara which reverberated across the mountains for several years, undeterred by the error but fuelled by the extreme devotion towards the divine. Valmiki became an enlightened soul because of the purity in his heart despite reciting the wrong mantra.

When the heart is pure and filled with devotion, even the wrong Mantra would sound like the most profound word for the divine, and he would bless the soul. This shows that the real faith is the one inside.

Valmiki in Penance (Fig 2.6)

## <u>Shams - Rule 17</u>

**The whole universe is contained within a single human being - You.** *Everything that you see around, including the things that you might not be fond of and even the people you despise or abhor, is present within you in varying degrees. Therefore, do not look for Shaitan (devil) outside yourself either. The devil is not an extraordinary force that attacks from without. It is an ordinary voice within. If you set to know yourself fully, facing with honesty and hardness.*

The above highlighted phrase, reminds me of *'Tat Tvam Asi'*, a phrase from Chandogya Upanishad which mean *Thou art That* (That you are). It reflects the innate connection of Universe and us. This profound concept is shown by Little Krishna as a playful little boy. Baby Krishna starts eating mud, a worried Balaram his elder brother, runs to inform Krishna's foster mother Yashoda, who comes in a hurry and asks Krishna to open his mouth. Krishna refuses to open his mouth initially but after she reprimands him severely and threatens to beat him up, he opens his mouth and she sees the entire universe inside the little boy. Yashodha faints on seeing this vision.

Lord Krishna showed that he is the Supreme Being but it also conveyed a subtle message. He swallowed a piece of earth in his mouth which reflected the universe. We are the universe and universe is us. In other words everything is connected.

In the second part of the rule Shams talks about the devil not being outside but from within. This very concept is explained in Sanathana Dharma through the traits that are inherent within the human body. We have three fundamental traits Sattva, Rajas and Tamas.

**Sattva** is centred around goodness, calmness and harmony.

**Rajas** is centred around activity, passion and movement.

**40**

**Tamas** is centred around Negligence, indolence and sleep.

The three remaining in equilibrium is the state of bliss. Unfortunately for humans these traits are not same across all individuals hence we have the good, the bad and the ugly around us. However there is a small portion of bad and ugly even in the extremely good person just that it doesn't manifest itself.

The ideal state of eternal bliss is to become completely Sattvik in nature where we are able to understand the true consciousness within us and do away with Rajas and Tamas.

As Brihadaranyaka Upanishad (Hindu scriptures that explain Vedas) says

*'Thamasoma Jyothirgamaya'* – Lead us from darkness to light

Universe inside Krishna (Fig 2.7)

## <u>Shams - Rule 18</u>

**If you want to change the ways others treat you, you should first change the way you treat yourself,** *fully and sincerely, otherwise there is no way you can be loved. Once you achieve that stage, however, be thankful for every thorn that others might throw at you. It is a sign that you will soon be showered in roses.*

The story of Pingala as stated in the Bhagwatham is a great example to illustrate the Sufi rule above. Pingala was a wealthy prostitute, she once befriended an extremely wealthy man and promised him that she wouldn't take anyone in that night. She decked herself in such a way that she was so attractive that everyone's jaw dropped when she stood near the doorway. Many men approached her and she shooed them away waiting for the wealthy man. The evening turned into night and soon it was close to midnight.

A moment of truth arose in her. I am wasting my time seeking pleasure for this body which is made of skin, bones and hair and excretes dirty things and will burn to ashes anyway. I have wasted my time on people who are not interested in me, but only this flesh. I have been waiting for one man who would give me wealth but forgot about the man who is in my heart who is making me function and who would give me the most invaluable wealth, which is salvation. From that very moment she dedicated her life to Lord Krishna and became a sage. The person who was being abused by the entire society soon became a Guru to several learned men.

It only takes a second for us to realize the truth. That moment will happen when we look at the way we treat ourselves with all sincerity and ask the question. Am I really happy with what I am doing to myself?

Pingala – Prostitute to Parama Bhakta (Fig 2.8)

## Shams - Rule 19

**Fret not where the road will take you.** *Instead concentrate on the first step. That is the hardest part and that is what you are responsible for. Once you take that step let everything do what it naturally does and the rest will follow. Don't go with the flow. Be the flow.*

This is one of my favourite Sufi rules, being the flow and not going with the flow. The hardest part is the first step, whether it's learning to sit, stand, walk, run, creating a business or plunging into spirituality. Once that is done, then you create the path.

The rule is epitomized by Lord Rama, The Prince of Ayodhya. Rama had very lofty ideals. Rama's principles were considered to be the ideal for any society and if the society functioned by following his principles to the T, Rama Rajya (Kingdom of Ram) is said to have arrived.

Dasharath, the King of Ayodhya, with a lot of pain in his heart grants two boons to his beloved wife Kaikeyi. He had given her a promise of two boons, when she had helped him in the war against the Asuras.

Dasharath is completely heart broken and doesn't want to face Rama his eldest son from his first wife Kausalya. Kaykeyi takes it upon herself to convey the message to Rama.

By the first boon, Rama would have to relinquish the throne for Kaikeyi's son and step brother Bharatha and by the second boon, he would have to go to the forest and live there for fourteen years. Rama didn't flinch, he bowed to his step mother and said he would leave at the earliest. Rama didn't worry about the future, he was in the here and now. Rama didn't worry about getting his Kingdom back. Rama didn't know whether he would survive fourteen years in the forest. He just left. When he was in the forest he lost his wife, who got kidnapped and he went in search of her. Rama just moved forward creating his own path. The path that all of us follow even today. The path of Rama which is called Ramayana. He didn't go with the flow, which would have been to challenge Bharatha to a war as a normal Kshatriya would do. He became the flow. The flow that is nurturing us even today after several thousands of years.

It is not good enough to just pray to Rama at home or go to his temple like a routine visit. It is important to follow the path of Rama and becoming the path ourselves for the future generations to follow.

Rama leaving Ayodhya (Fig 2.9)

## Shams - Rule 20

**We were all created in His image,** *and* **yet we were each created different and unique.** *No two people are alike. No hearts beat to the same rhythm. If God had wanted everyone to be the same, He would have made it so. Therefore, disrespecting differences and imposing your thoughts on others amounts to disrespecting God's holy scheme.*

Sweets may be of different shapes and sizes but the underlying sweetness comes from Sugar. Each of us may like a particular sweet, it is akin to us being aligned to a particular way of worship but the ultimate aim remains the same for the soul beneath the body. Lord Krishna and Lord Rama have a significant presence in Sanathana Dharma. Both are incarnations of Lord Vishnu and are considered complete incarnations. Two incidents in each of their lives indicates how we are all manifestations of the Lord but yet we are all created different but the goal is one and the same that of Eternal Salvation or Moksha.

In the Rama Avatar (Incarnation), Rama performs the last rites of Jatayu (Vulture), who fought valiantly to save Rama's wife, Sita from the Kidnapper Ravana. Jatayu was given Moksha by Lord Rama. In the life of Krishna, an Elephant called Gajendra, had the habit of taking lotus from a pond daily and praying to Lord Vishnu, the protector. One day when he was taking the lotus from the pond, a crocodile catches his leg. Gajendra screams for help and Vishnu appears in his vehicle Garuda (Eagle) and hurls his Chakra (Serrated Wheel) that beheads the crocodile. Gajendra attains Moksha too. The coveted status that humans struggle to achieve in several births was attained by a Vulture and an Elephant.

Whether it's an earth worm or a heavenly creature both are manifestations of the supreme. We are a small speck in the gigantic pathway between the macrocosm and the microcosm, hence we should respect the diversity of the universe filled with *chit* ( one that is conscious) and *achit* (What is not conscious ) and not impose ourselves and our views on anything and anyone.

Jatayu Moksha

Gajendra Moksha

(Fig 3.0)

## Shams - Rule 21

**When a true lover of God goes into a tavern, the tavern becomes his chamber of prayer,** *but when a wine bibber goes into the same chamber, it becomes his tavern. In everything we do, it is our hearts that make the difference, not our outer appearance. Sufis do not judge other people on how they look or who they are. When a Sufi stares at someone, he keeps both eyes closed instead opens a third eye – the eye that sees the inner realm.*

In Hindu philosophy, the one with the third eye is Lord Shiva. The third eye represents the inner eye. A state of enlightenment.

The story of an ardent devotee of Lord Shiva, Thinnar who became Kannappa Nayanar, one of the most revered saints of the Shaivite sect is a tell-tale example of how the tavern becomes a prayer chamber. Thinnar was a hunter and when he was out hunting with his friends, he saw a Shiva Lingam (the Abstract form in which Lord Shiva is worshipped). He instantly became a devotee of Lord Shiva, however being a hunter he didn't know the tradition, method, and prayer rituals to be performed at a temple. Thinnar would carry mouth full of water and spit it on the Shiva Lingam, he would decorate the shiva lingam with leaves and flowers that he stuck in his hair and he would offer raw Boar meat to the Lord. This crude form of worship went on for a week. The Priest in the temple could not tolerate this blasphemy and prayed to Lord Shiva to teach Thinnar a lesson.

The next day when Thinnar reached the Temple, he found that one of the eyes of Lord Shiva was bleeding. Thinnar was overwhelmed with emotion and couldn't bear to see blood from the Lords eyes. He took out his arrow and plucked out his left eye and placed it on the Lingam. The bleeding on the lingam stopped but within minutes the other eye started bleeding. Thinnar didn't hesitate for a moment, he took his leg and kept it on the position of the right eye on the Lingam, so he would know where to place the eye and was about to Gorge out his right eye, when Lord Shiva appeared in person and blessed him. The word 'Kann' in Tamil language means eye. Thinnar became Kannappa Nayanar. The priest who was watching the incident fell at the hunters feet realizing his folly.

What matters is the devotion in the heart. Discussing about our daily routines or vacation plans instead of praying at the temple is more blasphemous than a drunkard coming to pray with true devotion.

Kannappa Nayanar (Fig 3.1)

## Shams - Rule 22

**Life is a temporary loan and this world is nothing but a sketchy imitation of Reality.** *Only children would mistake a toy for the real thing. And yet human beings either become infatuated with the toy or disrespectfully break it and throw it aside. In this life, stay away from all kinds of extremities, for they will destroy your inner balance. Sufis do not go to extremes. A Sufi always remains mild and moderate.*

The first line in the rule is the exact words used by one of the great Tamil poets of our time Kannadasan. In one of the movie songs he wrote **'Iraval Thanthavan Ketkinran Avan Vendaam Enraal Viduvana'** literally translating to the owner has come back to claim what is rightfully his, which you had borrowed from him, referring to the human life. The Advaitha Philosophy is a direct reflection of the above Sufi message that we live in a world of Maya or Make-Believe which we have misunderstood as reality.

Let's delve into the story of Ravana the Demon King, who ruled the entire world and was the main antagonist in the Ramayana, the Evil Head who had kidnapped Rama's wife.

Ravana performed severe penance to please Brahma, the creator. The extent of the penance was so intense that Brahma was extremely pleased and came in front of Ravana and asked him what he wished for.

Ravana without batting an eyelid said, 'I seek immortality.'

'There is no such thing as immortality once you have been created in this world, you will eventually have to die. As a learned brahman you know this well. Seek something else.' Replied Brahma.

Ravana modified his request believing he was smart and said, 'I will give you a list of living beings who cannot kill me, grant me that wish.'

Brahma was pleased he wouldn't have to go back empty handed from such an ardent devotee. He granted him the wish.

Ravana's list included Plants, Animals, Devas, Asuras, Nagas, Daityas and all the Gods. The one creature he missed was the Human. He was so consumed by power that he felt that a human could never ever harm him. He didn't envisage a super human could be born to kill him. Ravana was slayed by Rama. The story doesn't end there, even Rama who is an incarnation of Vishnu, the protector eventually dies and so does Krishna the other powerful incarnation.

Birth has happened, Death will happen. The time we have in between is what we call as Life. Having a balance between the material and spiritual is important as we traverse the journey called Life. Buddha calls it the middle-path.

Krishna explains about Birth and Death in the following Sloka in the Bhagwad Gita

*'Jātasya hi dhruvo mṛityur dhruvaṁ janma mṛitasya cha*

*tasmād aparihārye 'rthe na tvaṁ śhochitum arhasi'*

What is born will die, what has died will be born again, don't fret over the inevitable.

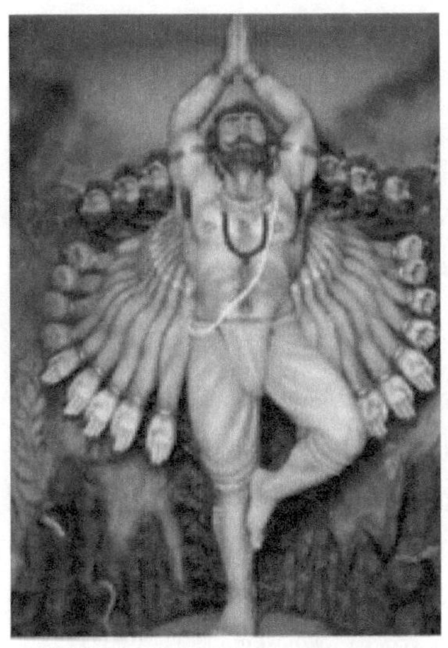

Ravana performing Penance (Fig 3.2)

**<u>Shams - Rule 23</u>**

**The human being has a unique place among God's creation.** *"I breathed into him of My Spirit," God says. Each and every one of us without exception is designed to be God's delegate on earth. Ask yourself, just how often do you behave like a delegate, if you ever do so? Remember, it falls upon each of us to discover the divine spirit inside and live by it.*

Krishna showcases this very aspect when he teaches Brahma a lesson. Brahma, the creator in the Hindu trinity had heard about Krishna's valour against the demons. He came to earth and saw a little Krishna eating butter and feeding other cowherds while their cows were grazing. Since he was the creator, he felt he should decide what happens to the creation and no one else, hence he kidnapped the cows and the cowherds and took them to Sathyalok which is Brahma's abode several billion light years away.

Brahma came back to earth to see the reaction to the calamity he had created. It was nearly a year on earth by the time he came back. Krishna, the cowherds, cows were all doing the exact same things as he had seen a year ago. Brahma was completely perplexed. He was unable to comprehend how things could be normal as they were earlier. Just as he was lost in thought, he heard bells from a temple nearby. To his utter amazement, there were several Brahma's worshipping the Lord. When realization dawned on him, he saw with his enhanced vision that Krishna was in every being whether it was the cow, cowherd, other celestial beings and even Brahma. He realized his folly and fell at Krishna's feet.

While God manifests himself in different forms. Humans are the only form with consciousness of all the creations. The purpose for creating us with consciousness was to enable us to understand the divinity that exists all around us and explore the subconscious mind that would connect us to the superconscious or the divine.

Brahma seeking Pardon ( Fig 3.3 )

### <u>Shams - Rule 24</u>

**Hell is in the here and now. So is heaven.** *Quit worrying about hell or dreaming about heaven, as they are both present inside this very moment. Every time we fall in love, we ascend to heaven. Every time we hate, envy or fight someone we tumble straight into the fires of hell.*

The Poignant story of Angulimala is a great example to illustrate the above rule. Angulimala was a dreaded dacoit who would plunder travellers and as a mark of his ruthlessness, he would cut off the little finger of the dead and wear it like a garland. Hence he got the name Angulimala (one with a garland of fingers). After a while the travellers stopped going in the route, he had 999 fingers in his garland, he just needed one more and he would have achieved his target. Angulimala grew restless, one day a monk was crossing through the woods. Angulimala desperately set after him to kill him and take his little finger for his garland. He could not catch up with the monk who was walking at a normal pace. After chasing the monk for a long time.

Angulimala called out to the monk and said, 'Stop Moving.'

The monk replied, 'I have stopped moving son, it is you who need to stop.'

'What do you mean,' asked Angulimala

The monk replied, 'My mind is at rest, you are yet to find peace of mind.'

'I don't need your preaching, I need your little finger,' screamed Angulimala.

The monk replied, ' if that gives you peace of mind, please take it.'

'I would have to kill you for that,' said Angulimala with disdain.

The monk replied, 'Please do so, son.'

Angulimala broke down on hearing this and fell at the monk's feet who was none other than Buddha.

Angulimala joined Buddha's group of mendicants and became a monk, serving his master, and tending to the sick.

One day he was seeking alms in a nearby town. When one of the merchants recognized him and raised an alarm. Soon a mob gathered. Angulimala was taking alms from a little boy and bent down to kiss him. As soon as Angulimala turned, he was pelted with stones. Severely beaten and bleeding he crawled towards his master. Buddha held him on his lap.

'I have finally found peace, I killed due to my ignorance and these people have also killed me because of their ignorance,' said Angulimala and collapsed.

Angulimala the Sinner became the Saint when he found True Love and Affection in Buddha. The Good People became the sinners when their minds were filled with hatred and revenge.

We are what we are in the here and now. If we are filled with love for people then we are the saint and if we are filled with hatred and envy, then we are the sinner.

***'Buddham Sharanam Gachami'*** (I go to The Buddha as my Refuge )

Angulimala chasing Buddha (Fig 3.4)

## Shams - Rule 25

**Each and every reader comprehends the Holy Qur'an on a different level of tandem with the depth of his understanding.** *There are four levels of insight. The first level is the outer meaning and it is the one that the majority of the people are content with. Next is the Batin – the inner level. Third, there is the inner of the inner. And the fourth level is so deep it cannot be put into words and is therefore bound to remain indescribable.*

The Bhagwad Gita is the equivalent of the Holy Qur'an from the perspective of the Hindus and Hinduism. Bhagwad Gita has several layers to it as well.

### The Parable

In a war between two cousins, the pandavas and the kauravas, the main warrior, the most powerful archer, Arjuna, who could decide the outcome of the war is in a state of depression and refuses to fight. He is not only a warrior but a very learned man as well. He believes it's pointless in killing his own grandfather, uncles, cousins, sons of relatives, family friends just for the sake of ruling over land. Fortunately for him his charioteer is Lord Krishna. Krishna explains to him the cycle of life and death, duty of his position and that the outcome of the war was not about him winning but restoring the path of righteousness or Dharma.

### The Inner Battle

The war is a metaphor for our own battles of what is right and wrong. Questioning the purpose of life, Our fear of death, Worrying about the future and not focusing on the present. Even a great warrior and a wise man like Arjuna was confused about his duties in the middle of a battle. We are mere mortals fighting the battle of life and more often than not forget our duties, let alone forget our duties, we forget who we are. We live in the illusion of light when we are in total darkness. We need a teacher to show us that light.

## The Song of God

We are so fickle in our mind that we get swayed by anything and everything. We use our intellect to interpret things and define our own rules and commandments and claim it to be the truth. We are a very small fry between the sub atomic and the sublime. We can't see below us and we can't see above us. The Lord himself decides to deliver a sermon that would be transferred down through generations for over five thousand years. The God reveals himself to all of us using Arjuna as the prop. He show us that he is Omnipotent (Having total authority), Omnipresent (Present everywhere) and Omniscient (Knowing everything). We need to simply follow whatever he has preached in the Bhagwad Gita as a subservient soul.

## The Real Purpose

The human being is the only conscious being on the earth and hence he has been delegated by god. We have to outgrow our animal instincts and figure out the real purpose in life which is to go back where we belong, the abode of god. The life that we live is temporary and not permanent and to find the real purpose of our life we need to look within, that is the reason we are bestowed with consciousness. Unfortunately, we have used it to look without and not within. The body has started controlling the mind rather than the other way around and we have become slaves to the body that will eventually decay and die. Bhagwad Gita is the holy scripture, which when read, understood, preached and practiced leads us to our inner light.

Every religion has a holy book. It needs to be approached with reverence. The state of our mind and body will determine how deep we go into it. When we delve deeper into the holy book, at some point in time, the transition will happen for every human being when he or she will transform from being an autobiography into becoming the holy book.

Bhagwad Gita (Fig 3.5)

**<u>Shams - Rule 26</u>**

**The universe is one being.** *Everything and everyone is interconnected through an invisible web of stories. Whether we are aware of it or not, we are all in a silent conversation. Do no harm. Practice compassion. And do not gossip behind anyone's back – not even a seemingly innocent remark! The words that come out of our mouths do not vanish but are perpetually stored in infinite space and they will come back to us in due time. One man's pain will hurt us all. One man's joy will make everyone smile.*

'We are all connected' is explained with this phrase form the Taittriya Upanishad,

*'Akashaat Vayuh, Vayur Agnihi, Agnire Apaha, Aadyah Pruthivi, Pruthivya Oshadhayaha, Oshadhayo Annam, Annaath Purushaha'*

From the Space comes the wind, from the wind comes fire, from fire comes water, from water comes earth, from earth comes vegetation, from vegetation comes food, from food comes human.

We are after all what we eat. The body has many sheaths within it and the first sheath is called *Annamaya Kosha*. The physical body which is kept alive by Annam or Food.

The *Pancha Bootha* or the five primordial elements that sustain all life are considered the manifestations of the Brahmam or the Supreme being. The beauty of the five primordial elements is that they are in a sequence matched with the number of attributes that they have.

**Akasha (Space)** - Space has only one attribute called Shabda (Sound). When we keep going up from earth into outer space there is total darkness and we can hear only sound.

**Vayuh (Wind)** – Wind has two attributes Shabda (Sound) and Sparsha (Touch). We can hear the wind and feel the wind.

**Agni (Fire)** – Fire has three attributes Shabda (Sound), Sparsha (Touch), Rupa (Form). We can hear the sound when Fire rages. We can touch fire and lastly we can see Fire daily through the day from morning till Sun set.

**Aapah (Water)** – Water has four attributes Shabda (Sound), Sparsha (Touch), Rupa (Form) and Rasa (Taste). We can hear the sound of the waves, flowing river, the rain. We touch water daily in some form or the other. We enjoy the water falls, the beauty of the sea, river and rain. We drink water and enjoy the natural taste of fresh water.

**Prithvi (Earth)** – Earth has five attributes Shabda (Sound), Sparsha (Touch), Rupa (Form), Rasa (Taste) and Gandha (Smell). The earth is full of sound and we hear it the most when we have the eruption of a Volcano or an Earth Quake. If the earth didn't have form, life wouldn't exist. Every root, shoot, stem, flower, fruit and vegetable we eat carries the taste of the earth. The smell of the earth is very profound when rain is in the air.

When we leave the earth, we are either burnt or buried depending on the custom we follow. We go back to where we came from.

Incidentally the human body is also *Pancha Bootha* which is represented by our five senses. The body which holds the organs is Space. The acid that burns our food and provides energy is fire, the air we breathe through our lungs and nostrils is wind. The blood that flows inside our body is water and the skin that covers us is the earth. It's not just coincidence that 3/4ths of the earth is water and 3/4ths of our body is water too.

In the Hindu custom, predominantly the body is burned in a wooden pyre placed on earth, pyre is lit so we are consumed by fire, the ashes are immersed in water (either in the sea or a river), when the ashes are thrown into the river some are carried by the wind and the departed soul is said to travel upwards into space.

All of us are the *Pancha Bootha* whether it's a single cell organism or the most evolved organism called human. Hence when we harm ourselves or harm someone with our senses or physically it will come back to us in some way because we are all connected. Let us receive the positive vibration from the flora, fauna around us and pass on the positive vibration to our fellow humans too.

Pancha Bhootha – Primordial Elements (Fig 3.6)

## <u>Shams - Rule 27</u>

**Whatever you speak, good or evil, will somehow come back to you.** *Therefore, if there is someone who harbours ill thoughts about you, saying similarly bad things about him will only make matters worse. You will be locked in a vicious circle of malevolent energy. Instead for forty days and nights say and think nice things about that person. Everything will be different at the end of 40 days, because you will be different inside.*

The story of Kumbhakarna, the brother of the mighty Ravana is a good example to explain the fact that we will be haunted by what we speak.

Just like Ravana, Kumbhakarna also took up a severe penance to please Brahma, the creator. The sworn enemy of the Asura clan that Kumbhakarna belonged to, were the Devas and the leader of the Devas was Indira.

Pleased with his penance, Lord Brahma asked Kumbhakarna to state his wish. He was about to ask for **Indra Asan** (Seat of Indra) indirectly meaning that he wished to be the leader of the Devas. In a slip of the tongue, he said **Nidra Asana** (Seat of Sleep). Brahma granted the boon to Kumbhakarna. Ravana became very displeased and asked Brahma to take back the boon. Once granted a boon couldn't be taken back, however brahma showed leniency and said that Kumbhakarna would be asleep six months of a year. It is said that Saraswathi, the Goddess of Learning caused the slip of the tongue to happen. The bottom-line, his own words came to haunt him.

If a powerful warrior and knowledgeable person like Kumbhakarna could become tongue-tied, we are ordinary mortals and we don't even need Goddess of knowledge to create the issue. We gloat on our ignorance and end up speaking many things in haste without understand that it would come back to haunt us.

The message has been reiterated across different eons of time. Kumbhakarna lived in the Treta Yuga. We live in the time period known as Kali Yuga, and in the 3$^{rd}$ century, one of the greatest Tamil poets, Thiruvalluvar through his treatise "Thirukkural" taught about **Aram** (Righteousness), **Porul** (Wealth generation or Economy) and **Inbam** (Desire). In one of the verses in the subsection on righteousness, he talks about controlling the tongue.

*'Yaakaavaa Raayinum Naakaakka Kaavaakkaal*

*Soakaappar Sollizhukkup Pattu'*

Whether you control anything else or not, control your tongue otherwise errors of speech and the consequent misery will ensue.

Khumbakarna's Curse (Fig 3.7)

## Shams - Rule 28

**The past is an interpretation. The future is an illusion.**
*The world does not move through time as if it were a straight line, proceeding from the past to the future. Instead time moves through and within us, in endless spirals. Eternity does not mean infinite time, but simply timelessness. If you want to experience eternal illumination, put the past and the future out of your mind and remain within the present moment.*

Arjuna refuses to fight in the Kurukshetra war due to the potential death of near and dear ones. He also felt it was pointless to rule over a kingdom on the dead bodies of his loved ones. Krishna gave the entire treatise of the Bhagwad Gita which has 700 verses across 18 chapters covering various aspects of Life and Death. One of the most famous verses from the Bhagwad Gita is the following

*'Karmanye Vadhikaraste Ma Phaleshu Kadachana,*

*Ma Karmaphalaheturbhurma Te Sangostvakarmani'*

You have the right to work only but never to its fruits.

Let not the fruits of action be your motive, nor let your attachment be to inaction.

He points to Arjuna that he is a Kshatriya (Warrior) who is in the middle of a warzone. The primary duty of a Kshatriya is to fight for the rights of his people and his kingdom. He goes onto say that Arjuna was focused on the outcome of the war which is the future and his inaction is due to attachment, which comes from the connections of the past.

His grandfather and guru who taught him are in front of him and he is brooding because of the past connection. Krishna says they are your enemy, this is a battlefield and you are a Kshatriya and do you your duty as a Kshatriya.

All of us have responsibilities in life, when we procrastinate, thinking about the past of **what could have been** and worrying about **what would be**, we forget to focus on the here and now.

We should detach ourselves from the past and future as neither of it would change just by thinking about it. Detaching from the past and future, gives us the freedom to act with purpose in the present, bringing focus into our actions that could produce the best results.

Focus on Duty not on Outcome (Fig 3.8)

## <u>Shams -Rule 29</u>

**Destiny doesn't mean that your life has been strictly predetermined.** *Therefore, to leave everything to the fate and to not actively contribute to the music of the universe is a sign of sheer ignorance. The music of the universe is all pervading and it is composed on 40 different levels. Your destiny is the level where you play your tune. You might not change your instrument but how well to play is entirely in your hands.*

Let us look at two women who took their challenge head-on instead of brooding over their fate. Savithri and Gandhari. Their examples reflect the above Sufi rule that you can create your own destiny and not leave things to fate.

Savithri was the daughter of Ashvapathi, the King of Madra. Savitri was so beautiful that no one dared to ask for her hand in marriage. Ashvapathi asked her to choose her husband. After travelling through hermitages, she returned to Madra. She informed her father that she had chosen an exiled prince, Sathyavan as her husband. Sathyavan was destined to die in a year. Her father pleaded with her to change her choice but she stood firm. Three days before Sathyavan's death date, she started performing religious austerities. When Yama, the Lord of Death came to take away Sathyavan's soul, she followed Yama and argued with him about Truth, Righteousness, and Compassion. Pleased with her wisdom and her dedication, he granted several boons including the boon of begetting 100 sons, except Sathyavan's life. She finally argued that the virtuous who followed the path of truth would go to any extent to remain truthful. Yama was the King of Righteousness and hence his boons should be true in letter and spirit. Yama was stumped and gave her Sathyavan's life back. Savitri chose a path to which she was true till the end and rewrote fate and created her own destiny.

The second is that of Gandhari. Gandhari was born in the kingdom of Gandhar in the ancient Indian subcontinent. Bheeshma who was the custodian of the Kingdom of Kuru's was bestowed with the responsibility of finding a wife for the Blind Prince Dhirthirashtra. Bheeshma came to Gandhar and asked King Sulabha for the hand of his daughter, Gandhari for Dhirthirashtra. Gandhari agreed to the proposal for two main reasons. If Sulabha refused the offer, Bheeshma would anyway defeat him and take her captive as no one could defeat Bheeshma. Secondly Hastinapur kingdom was much larger than Gandhar. Gandhar would have a strategic advantage, if the families became relatives. Gandhari went onto wear a blind fold because her husband was blind. It was her way of showing her love and dedication to her husband. Instead of brooding and sulking over the situation. Gandhari chose to find meaning in a difficult situation. Gandhari was so highly regarded by Lord Krishna that he accepted her curse that his entire clan would be destroyed as he didn't stop the Kurukshetra war even though he could.

We can't change where we are born or how we are born but what we become is entirely in our hands. This body itself is a miracle and our conscious within this body is an even bigger miracle. Understanding this miracle and using it for short lived pleasures or exalted purposes is up to us.

Savitri and Gandhari – Finding Purpose in Adversity (Fig 3.9)

## <u>Shams - Rule 30</u>

**The true Sufi is such that even when he is unjustly accused, attacked and condemned** *from all sides, he* **patiently endures,** *uttering not a single bad word about any of his critics. A Sufi never apportions blame. How can there be opponents or rivals or even "others" when there is no "self" in the first place? How can there be any one to blame when there is only One?*

Going back to the story of Prahalad. He believed Hari was the supreme being and everything is the manifestation of Hari and kept reciting his name "Narayana Narayana" (Lord Vishnu) all the time . Hiranyakashipu who was his father and demon King accused Prahlad of being a traitor as he wasn't willing to accept that Hiranyakashipu was the greatest. Hiranyakashipu threatened him with dire consequences, if he didn't mend his ways. Prahlad did not flinch and continued his undeterred faith of the Brahman or Supreme being. Reasoning failed, Threat failed and Hiranyakashipu felt there was no other option than to kill his son who was a deviant.

He first asked that he be trampled by the fiercest elephant in the Kingdom. The elephant instead of trampling him garlanded Prahlad. The King was enraged further and decided to throw him from the mountain top, Prahlad survived without even a scratch. His hands and legs were tied and he was thrown into the sea. He survived that too. He was finally poisoned even then he didn't die. Through all of this ordeal Prahlad did not utter one word against his father. He always believed "His Hari" will transform his father one day.

In Hindu philosophy, the Supreme Being is understood in two ways. Saguna Brahmam and Nirguna Brahmam. Saguna Brahmam is the Brahmam that is considered to have form and shape as seen by Prahlada. Nirguna Brahmam is formless and is the core component of Advaita Philosophy propagated by Adi Shankara as the only truth. In whichever way we decide to look at the Brahmam, if we do it with utmost faith and deep devotion to the Brahmam, We will perceive the good, bad and the ugly in the same way.

A line from a film song by the great Tamil poet Kannadasan sums it all up

*'Potruvaar Potralum Thootruvaar Thootralum Pogattum Kannanukke'*

I place all the bouquets and the brickbats at the feet of Lord Krishna.

Prahlad's Endurance (Fig 4.0)

## <u>Shams - Rule 31</u>

**If you want to strengthen your faith, you will need to soften inside.** *For your faith to be rock solid, your heart needs to be as soft as a feather. Through an illness, accident, loss or fright, one way or another, we are all faced with incidents that teach us how to become less selfish and judgmental and more compassionate and generous. Yet some of us learn the lesson and manage to become milder, while some others end up becoming even harsher than before...*

Kamba Ramayanam is the Tamil Version of the great Hindu Epic the Ramayana. In the Kishkindha Kaandam or Chapter of Kiskhinda, there is a poignant scene where the dying Vaali, the Monkey King speaks to Rama his vanquisher, the Incarnation of Lord Vishnu. Vaali had usurped the Kingdom from his brother Sugreeva and had Kidnapped his wife Ruma as well. The conversation of Vaali and Rama is as below,

'You have killed me in haste. I would have brought Ravana and thrown him at your feet,' said Vaali.

'Vaali, I have not killed you, I have liberated you,' replied Rama.

Vaali realized that he had turned a Tyrant and was following the path of Adharma (Unrighteousness) and it was important for him to be eliminated for the good of their clan, The Vaanara.

At that moment, he called Angad his son and told him, Rama is everything to you now. Simply follow everything that he says blindly. Before breathing his last, Vaali tells Rama, even if Sugreeva commits any blunder, he should be pardoned as he wouldn't be able to withstand Rama's force. He says this knowing fully well that Sugreeva had orchestrated his murder at the hands of Rama.

Vaali in the presence of Rama, went from a tyrant to one with a tender heart. Proximity to the Supreme Being, had purified his soul.

The Vishnu Sahasranama that describes the 1000 names of Lord Vishnu describes this quality of Vishnu in a beautiful verse

*'Pavithranam Pavithram yo mangalanam cha mangalam*

*Dhaivatham devathanam cha bhootanam yo vya pitha'*

The Purest of the Pure, The most auspicious of the auspicious, he is the god of gods and indestructible father of all the beings.

The perspective of many people changed post the Covid-19 pandemic where lives were lost in millions, it did soften the hearts of many. We don't need to wait for death to build faith in the divine, we can do it while alive by simply seeing Goodness and Godness around us with a gentle heart.

Rama consoling Vaali (Fig 4.1)

## Shams -Rule 32

**Nothing should stand between you and God.** *No imams, priests, rabbits or any other custodians of moral or religious leadership. Not spiritual masters and not even your faith. Believe in your values and your rules, but never lord them over others. If you keep breaking other people's hearts, whatever religious duty you perform is no good. Stay away from all sorts of idolatry, for they will blur your vision. Let God and only God be your guide. Learn the Truth, my friend, but be careful not to make a fetish out of your truths.*

This is the very basis of Sanathana Dharma. While there are sects and subsects, various rituals and multiple methods of worship, each one choses his or her own method that suits them as devotion is a one-to-one communication between the Brahmam and us. This is explained through the story of Adishankara that is captured in the book Shankara Digvijaya ( Autobiography of Adi Shankara ).

One day Adi Shankara was performing mid-day ablutions in the Ganges in the city of Kashi and walking towards a temple. He was accosted by a Chandala with four dogs. Chandala were the people who disposed off dead bodies by burning them. Adi Shankara asked him to move away as per the prevailing custom in those days as they were untouchables. The Chandala in reply said, "O Great Sage which one of me do you want me to move. My body or my soul. If it's my body, you and I eat the same food so there is no difference between you and me. The soul is pure and is a part of the Brahman so it doesn't differentiate."

Adishankara immediately fell down at the Chandala's feet as he had shown him the mirror that reflected his own philosophy, Advaitha Vedanta which prophesised that except the Brahmam everything else is illusion. There is a version that the Chandala turned about to Lord Shiva. It doesn't really matter if he was Shiva or Shivam, a state of being like Shiva or Stateless, the story showed that even an enlightened soul could be blinded when the rules lord over them.

If Adi Shankara himself could have a moment of blindness when sucked into the realm of rules and methods, we are but mere mortals. It is important to understand the rules, methods and rituals of the sect you are part of and If possible practice it too, but it should not override the premise that unless you have compassion in your heart and detachment from your body you will not experience the Brahmam or the Only Truth.

Adishankara encounters a Chandala (Fig 4.2)

### <u>Shams - Rule 33</u>

**While everyone in this world strives to get somewhere and become someone, only to leave it all behind after death**. *You aim for the supreme stage of nothingness. Live this life as light and empty as the number zero. We are no different from a pot. It is not the decorations outside but the emptiness inside that holds us straight. Just like that, it is not what we aspire to achieve but the consciousness of nothingness that keeps us going.*

The example that immediately comes to my mind for the above rule is the statement by one of the most renowned Siddhars. The term "Siddha" is used in Indian religions and culture to describe a perfected master, one who has achieved a high degree of perfection of the intellect and liberation or enlightenment. The state of enlightenment is called "Siddhi" and the enlightened one is called a "Siddhar".

Pattinathar, a Siddhar who lived in the $14^{th}$ century is said to have been transformed after he receives a divine note which reads

*'Kaathatra Oosiyum Vaarathu Kaan Kadai Vazhikke'*

It says, even a needle with a broken eye will not accompany you when you leave.

We live in a world where we constantly keep running to attain more and more to fulfil our aspirations. We gain tremendous material wealth and in the process lose our health. We do not realize, that nothing would come with us, when it is time for us to leave. Even the progeny for whom we may be accumulating the mountains of wealth, may or may not utilize the wealth in the right way, we wouldn't be around to see it too. It is important to have material wealth to sustain in this world but to sustain our soul, we need to build spiritual wealth which can only be attained by looking within.

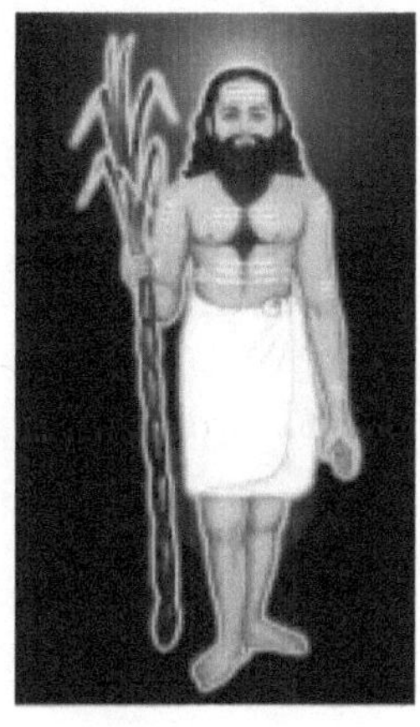

Pattinathar

(Fig 4.3)

## Shams - Rule 34

**Submission does not mean being weak or passive.** *It leads to neither fatalism nor capitulation. Just the opposite. True power resides in submission - a power that comes from within. Those who submit to the divine essence of life will live in unperturbed tranquillity and peace even the whole wide world goes through turbulence after turbulence.*

The above rule is reflected by one word in Sanathana Dharma which is "Sharanagathi" which means to surrender completely to the will of the divine.

Krishna in the charama shloka from the Gita states unambiguously the path to the salvation. Charama in Sanskrit means the ultimate or final.

*'Sarva-dharmān parityajya mām ekaṁ śharaṇaṁ vraja*

*ahaṁ tvāṁ sarva-pāpebhyo mokṣ hayiṣ hyāmi mā śhuchaḥ'*

Abandon all varieties of dharmas and simply surrender unto Me alone. I shall liberate you from all sinful reactions; do not fear.

Throughout the entire treatise of Bhagwad Gita, Krishna had been preaching to Arjuna to follow the Dharma. In the final Shloka he says abandon all Dharma and simply surrender unto me alone. It is like a googly, to use an analogy from cricket. The explanation of the shloka is deeper. Till now Krishna was telling Arjuna to do the duties that is associated with his position which is that of a Kshatriya, now he is referring to the duty of the Aathma or Soul which is total surrender to the supreme. It is known as Para Dharma. Dharma of the Aathma towards the Paramathma.

To completely submit to the will of the divine takes tremendous courage. It is not a sign of weakness but a sign of great strength. When we understand and follow Para Bhakti or unwavering devotion to the divine, we receive Para Gnana or the Knowledge of the Divine. The knowledge of the divine leads us to Para dharma known as Sharanagathi.

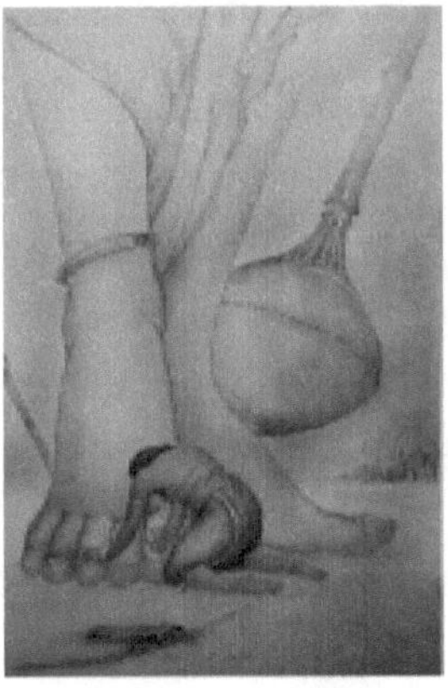

Sharanagathi – Total Surrender (Fig 4.4)

## <u>Shams -Rule 35</u>

**In this world, it is not similarities or regularities that take us a step forward, but blunt opposites**. *And all the opposites in the universe are present within each and every one of us. Therefore the believer needs to meet the unbeliever residing within. And the nonbeliever should get to know the silent faithful in him. Until the day one reaches the stage of Insane-I Kamil, the perfect human being, faith is a gradual process and one that necessitates its seeming opposite: disbelief.*

Matter in science is referred to as an object that has mass and occupies space. If I keep an object next to you, you are able to see it, if I keep it at a distance you are able to partially see it. If I take it out of your sight it becomes invisible. Let us integrate this analogy back to the concept of faith and disbelief.

Kannadasan the renowned Poet says it all, with the below phrase

*"Kal endraal athu Kal Dhaan, Deivam endraal athu Deivam"*

If it's a stone it's a stone, if it's God it's God

One sees Divinity in the Stone and the other sees only a Stone. Denial doesn't mean it is not there. As seen above the object was there, now it is not there as it was moved. The underlying message is that you can only deny something that is there, you cannot deny something which doesn't exist. Science also says opposites attract. What are clearly polar opposites attract each other and this constant friction which mould us eventually.

Science is an activity that relates to the brain and Faith is an activity that relates to the heart. Science ends with faith and Religion begins with faith. When the brain and heart come to a perfect harmony, we will understand the science of the sublime. This is precisely what Lord Krishna says through two verses in the Bhagwad Gita.

*'Chatur-vidhā bhajante mām janāḥ sukṛitino 'rjuna*

*ārto jijñāsur arthārthī jñānī cha bharataṛ habha'*

O best amongst the Bharatas, four kinds of people engage in My devotion—the distressed, the seekers of knowledge, the seekers of worldly possessions, and those who are situated in knowledge.

Krishna sees four different types of devotees that reach out to him. The first are the ones in distress. They can't find solution to their problems, so they call up the divine to find answers. The second are those who want to expand their knowledge from the worldly matters to spiritual matters. The third are those who wish for prosperity in the world. The final ones are those who seek him as they are in search of the ultimate truth. Krishna follows up the above verse with this next one.

*'Teṣ hām jñānī nitya-yukta eka-bhaktir viśhiṣ hyate*

*priyo hi jñānino 'tyartham ahaṁ sa cha mama Priyaḥ'*

Amongst these, I consider them to be the highest, who worship Me with knowledge, and are steadfast in their devotion and seek only Me. I am very dear to them and they are very dear to Me.

Krishna clearly points out the seekers of paramātmā as the ultimate truth are the true gnani and they are dearest to him.

Even within the believers we need to transcend from the state of using God as an errand boy or a genie to solve our day-to-day problems in life, to seeking him out as the only wealth that matters. The non-believers are in a state of constant denial as they forever try to rationalize every aspect of life. They too reach a dead end. Science and Scientists can't explain every single phenomenon.

We constantly move between the two states of belief and disbelief depending upon our personal and emotional needs being satisfied. We need to have this constant friction to eventually transform into the state of a "Gnani".

Polar Opposites (Fig 4.5)

## <u>Shams - Rule 36</u>

**This world is erected upon the principle of reciprocity**. *Neither a drop of kindness nor a speck of evil will remain unreciprocated. For not the plots, deceptions, or tricks of other people. If somebody is setting a trap, remember, so is God. He is the biggest plotter. Not even a leaf stirs outside God's knowledge. Simply and fully believe in that. Whatever God does, He does it beautifully.*

Lord Rama brought Ahalya back from her curse of being turned into a stone. He also killed Tharaka, a demonic women. Rama provided deliverance both ways, curing the curse of a pious women who was a victim of circumstance and gave another women a better life than the demonic way, by killing her body.

Lord Krishna, buy moving the mortar stone between the Arjuna trees liberated the two celestial beings Nalakuvara and Manigriva from their curse. He also plotted the downfall of Bheeshma, Drona and Karna in the Kurukshetra war. In the first case, he relieved them from the curse as they had served time. In the latter, he was the key strategist in the Dharmic war to establish righteousness.

Every act of kindness, deliverance and death are plotted by the Supreme Being. We just don't know it unless we experience it. This concept of God driving everything that happens around us is explained in the below Shloka from Vishnu Sahasranamam, a religious text written by Veda Vyasa in the Mahabharata.

*'Udbhavah ksho-bhano devah shree-garbhah parame-shvarah
|*

*Karanam kaaranam kartha vikartha gahano guhah ||'*

In the first line. Lord Vishnu is defined as The origin of the universe, The Creator of Commotion, The Supreme being, The one who protects Lakshmi (Goddess of wealth) and one who has all the auspicious qualities within him.

In the second line, he is defined as Karanam – The Means , Kaaranam – The Cause , Kartha – The doer , Vikartha – The Change Agent, Gahanaha – The deep and inscrutable and lastly Guhah – The one who is hidden.

Lord is always hidden unless we completely surrender to him. Because he is invisible, we believe we are the plotters of good and bad deeds. He is always watching, observing, and plotting in his own way and he reciprocates at the appropriate time. We just need to understand there is an invisible hand at work.

Deliverance by Rama and Krishna (Fig 4.6)

## Shams - Rule 37

**God is a meticulous clock maker.** *So precise is His order that everything on earth happens in its own time. Neither a minute late nor a minute early. And for everyone without exception, the clock works accurately. For each there is a time to love and a time to die.*

In Sanathana Dharma there are two concepts called **Srishti** which means creation and **Pralaya** which means destruction. It follows a cyclical pattern, one follows the other. The manifestation of Vishnu is Srishti which includes the system of the universe, flora, fauna and humans. When the appropriate time comes, there is Pralaya where Lord Vishnu unmanifests them back on to himself.

The Vishwa Roopam or Virata Roopam is the gigantic form of Lord Vishnu where everything to do with **Prakruthi**, the universe, The Celestial beings and Gods are all represented in a single form. In the Mahabharata, Arjuna is shown this form to make him understand, that it is the Supreme being who is delivering the sermon to him. It was also to show him that life and death both are God's making and within him and there is nothing that is separate from him.

The last line of the Sufi rule can be very subtly represented by the life of Lord Krishna himself. There was a time when he was fully in love and inseparable from Radha and there was a time when he himself dies to bring an end to the Dvapara Yuga and start the Kali Yuga. Each Yuga represents a certain eon of time. The Lord shows that there is a time and place for everything, even for the Supreme Being. Hence he knows when it is time for us.

Cycle of Life within him

Krishna's time to Leave

(Fig 4.7)

### <u>Shams - Rule 38</u>

**It is never too late to ask yourself, "Am I ready to change the life I am living?** *Am I ready to change within?" Even if a single day in your life is the same as the day before, it surely is a pity. At every moment and with each new breath, one should be renewed and renewed again. There is only one-way to be born into a new life: to die before death.*

Lord Rama was asked to go for Vanavaas or Living in the forest for fourteen years, he accepted his step-mothers' ask and donned the robes of a hermit and moved on, he ceased to be a prince the moment he stepped out of the palace both physically and mentally and became a hermit in body and mind. Lord Krishna provided the sermon on the duties of a Kshatriya to Arjuna but left the decision to him, if he wanted to fight the battle or continue to sulk and run away from war. Arjuna was ready to change from within and transformed from Hermit to a Kshatriya and won the war for the Pandavas.

The two great preachers of the Land, Adi Shankara and Siddhartha Gautama both focused on the inner light. This inner light could only be achieved by the willingness to change. Adi Shankara asked people to differentiate between their illusion and the real truth. It takes tremendous courage, tenacity and conviction to deem all the worldly pleasures as illusion. Buddha believed that the root cause of all misery was desire, so a monastic way of life away from this desire would help the man focus his energies in seeking the truth.

Adoption and Adaption has helped the human to evolve from the apes to homo sapiens. This adoption was for survival and when the willingness to seek the divine by renewing oneself every day is adopted as the way of life, death just seems another stop in the spiritual journey.

Prince to Hermit (Rama)

Hermit to Prince (Arjuna)

(Fig 4.8)

<u>**Shams - Rule 39**</u>

**While the parts change, the whole always remains the same**. *For every thief who departs this world, a new one is born. And every decent person who passes away is replaced by a new one. In this way not only does nothing remain the same but also nothing ever really changes. For every Sufi who dies, another is born somewhere.*

In the Hindu scriptures, There is the story of a demon called Raktha Bija meaning Blood Seed. Every time blood drops on the ground another demon rises. Goddess Kali is the ferocious form of Lord Shakti, the feminine power centre. She sucks the blood out of Raktha Bija and ensure it stays with her. This is the most common imagery of Kali to depict this incident, it shows her holding a skull in her hand and her tongue jutting out. In our world we will find there are so many Raktha Bija's created every day and destroyed every day.

In the Sri Vaishnava tradition. We believe in the concept of a Guru Lineage that enables people to understand Bhakthi and experience the divine. It starts with Lakshmi Nathan in other words Lord Vishnu and goes down to the Azhwars, 12 Vaishnavite saints who propagated Vaishnavism, followed by the Acharya or Guru such as Nadhamuni, Yamunacharya, Ramanujacharya and Vedanta Desikar. Ramanuja further established 74 centres and Heads who would continue to propagate the divine knowledge. This seed of Knowledge is continuing even now and will continue in the future generation too.

Koorathaazhwan, the foremost Disciple of Ramanujacharya wrote the below Shloka which depicts the Guru Parampara or Lineage

*'LakshminAtha samarambhAm natha yamuna madhyamam*

*asmadhacharya paryantham vandhe guru paramparam'*

I worship the glorious Guru Parampara which starts with Sriman Narayanan, has Nathamuni and Yamunacharya in the middle and ends with my Aacharyan (Ramanuja). I pay my obeisance to this Guru Lineage.

Ramanujacharya in his teaching says both the seeds of good and bad reside inside us, whatever we decide to nurture will grow. When you spend the time in devotion towards the divine, the good seed gets nurtured and eventually will blossom with the experience of the divine.

Kali – Raktha Bija

Azhwar-Acharya Parampara

(Fig 4.9)

## Shams - Rule 40

**A life without love is of no account**. *Don't ask yourself what kind of love you should seek, spiritual or material, divine or mundane, Eastern or Western. Divisions only lead to more divisions. Love has no labels, no definitions. It is what it is, pure and simple. Love is the water of life. And a lover is a soul of fire! The universe turns differently when fire loves water..*

Whether it's the uninhibited love of the Azhwars towards Sriman Narayana including Andal the young girl who wanted to marry Lord Vishnu or the Nayanmaars, the Shaivite saints who were lost permanently in the love of Lord Shiva, both show that there is no greater attribute than love. There are two profound sets of verses from saints of both sects that emphasizes the power of true love.

*'Anbe Thagaliya Aarvame NeyyAga*

*Inburugu Sindhai Idhu ThiriyA Nanburugi*

*Gyanach Chudar Vilakku Errinen Naarranaruku*

*Gyanath Thamizh Purindha Naan'*

The above verses are part of the Divyaprabhandam, the sacred Vaishnavite text that has poems from all the Azhwars. This set of verses is sung by Boodhathu Azhwar considered to be the second Azhwar in the lineage of Azhwars.

Anbu in Tamil means Love, he says I will use my love of god as the lamp, my bhakti or devotion to him as ghee (clarified butter), my mind which is filled with happiness to see the

Lord as the wick, my soul that is melting at the thought of the lord and light the lamp of knowledge to Lord Narayana. In the last line he praises the language Tamil that helped earn this knowledge. You need a base to hold the oil, wick and the fire, that base is Love says Boodhathu Azhwar.

*'Anbum Sivamum irandu enbar arivilaar*

*Anbe Sivam aavadu yaarum arikilaar*

*Anbe Sivam aavadu yaarum arindapin*

*Anbe Sivam aai amarndu irundaare.' [Thirumanthiram]*

The above poem is part of Thirumanthirum, a set of 3000 texts which forms a part of Thirumarai, the compilation of different Nayanmaars which forms the basis of the Shaiva Siddhanta Philosophy or Shaivism where Shiva is considered the supreme lord. Thirumanthirum is written by Thirumoolar, one of the 63 Nayanmaars, and also considered as a Siddhar( Enlightened One).

Thirumoolar says, Fools believe that Love and Shiva are two different aspects. People don't realize Love is god, when they realize that Love is God, they will themselves reach the state of Shivam.

The two major saints of Vaishnavite and Shaivite sect which form the majority of Sanathana Dharma have clearly articulated that once we find true love, one will see Godliness in everything and everyone.

Bhoodathaazwar

Thirumoolar (Fig 5.0)

As the threads of Sufism and Sanathana intertwine, a breathtaking tapestry unfolds, showcasing timeless spiritual wisdom. Within its vibrant contours, Love, Devotion, Empathy, and Selflessness converge, held together by the central core – the Supreme Being.

The Supreme Being is revered in many ways as diverse forms, as formless, as pure light, and the ultimate truth. Despite the diversity of the paths, the underlying truth remains constant, as illuminated by this confluence of philosophies. Spirituality is a personal journey, a one-to-one communion between the disciple and the Divine. If we continue the journey with dedication in the mind and devotion in our heart, we will surely experience the divine.

# Illustration Credits

**Shams - Rule - 1**

Fig 1.1 : Narasimha killing Hiranyakashipu – Courtesy of Wikipedia

**Shams - Rule - 2**

Fig 1.2 : Radha and Krishna – Courtesy of Pinterest

**Shams – Rule – 3**

Fig 1.3 : Vamana – Courtesy of Pinterest

**Shams – Rule – 4**

Fig 1.4 : Arjuna & Duryodhana with Krishna – Courtesy of Pinterest

Fig 1.4 : Krishna saving Draupadi's chastity – Courtesy of Quora

**Shams – Rule – 5**

Fig 1.5 : Krishna & Sudama – Courtesy of Jagran ( jagran.com)

**Shams – Rule – 6**

Fig 1.6 : Shabari & Rama – Courtesy of Pinterest

**Shams – Rule – 7**

Fig 1.7 : Kunti – Curtesy of Jiva.org

**Shams – Rule – 8**

Fig 1.8 : Sita & Hanuman – Courtesy of Pinterest

**Shams – Rule – 9**

Fig 1.9 : Adishankara – Courtesy of Wikipedia

Fig 1.9 : Ramana Maharishi – Courtesy of Ekatma.org

**Shams – Rule – 10**

Fig 2.0 : Arjuna in Distress – Courtesy of hinducosmos.com

# Glossary

**Advaita** – The philosophy that purports non-duality of soul and the supreme

(Brahmam)

**Avatar** – Incarnation of God

**Bhakti** – Devotional Love

**Dasavatharam** – Ten incarnations of Lord Vishnu, The Preserver

**Dvaita** – The Philosophy that purports that God and individual souls exist in independent realities with the soul dependent on God

**Dvapara Yuga** – Third Age of the world cycle as per Hindu Scriptures

**Gopikas** – Devotees and Consorts of Lord Krishna

**Jiva** – Soul

**Kali Yuga** – The Final Age of the world cycle as per Hindu Scriptures

**Karma** – Action and its consequences

**Kritha Yuga** – First Age of the world cycle as per Hindu Scriptures

**Lingam** – A sign, symbol or Mark of God & God's power

**Moksha** – Liberation from the cycle of death and rebirth

**Sanathana Dharma** – Eternal Law or Eternal Order

**Sufi** – Mystical Islamic practice that focuses on spirituality

**Treta Yuga** – Second Age of the world cycle as per Hindu Scriptures

**Upanishad** – Later Hindu Scriptures after Vedas that focus on Philosophical thoughts for spiritual enlightenment

**Visishtadvaita** – The philosophy that purports non-duality with distinctions. It accepts Brahmam is supreme while also acknowledging its multiplicity

**Yuga** – An age of Time

# Bibliography


1. Forty Rules of Love – Elif Shafak
2. Sufi Path of Love - Forty rules of love of Shams of Tabriz 1185-1248
3. Bhagavad Gita
4. Upanishads
5. Vishnu Sahasranamam
6. Divya Prabhandam
7. Upadesha Sahasri
8. Thirumanthiram
9. Shankara Digvijaya
10. Kannadasan songs